FOR MY DAD, JOSEPH PROVOST, AND MY
HERD: STEVE, NOELLE, AND CAYMAN – KT

THE
ELEPHANTS COME HOME

A True Story of Seven Elephants, Two People, and One Extraordinary Friendship

Written by
KIM TOMSIC

Illustrated by
HADLEY HOOPER

chronicle books·san francisco

This is Françoise.
She loves Lawrence.

This is Lawrence.
He loves animals.

This is Max.

And this is **THULA THULA**—
a farmhouse, a garden, a swimming pool,
and 11,000 acres of African bush,
savanna, and forest.

Around Thula Thula stretch miles and miles of fences, so the rhinos can splash in the river.

The impala, Cape buffalo, and zebra can graze the savanna.
Even the crocodiles at the Gwala Gwala dam can swim in peace.

There is **NO HUNTING** at Thula Thula.

When spitting snakes creep into the farmhouse kitchen,
Lawrence uses a soft broom to scoot them outside.

When bark spiders weave webs
between the patio furniture,

Françoise tiptoes around them.

And when monkeys steal cheese from
Françoise and treats from Max, well,

it's a monkey's job to find
food, so nobody scolds them.

One day a lady telephones.

"Lawrence," she says. "Will you adopt a herd of angry elephants?"

"Angry?" Lawrence asks.

"They've been **BULLIED** and **HUNTED**," the lady says. "Now they roar at the rangers and crush our fences. Folks are frightened the herd might stampede through town. The village chief says it's a matter of safety—the herd must leave or be shot."

Lawrence has never taken care of elephants, but he says, yes, they may come to Thula Thula.

To prepare for their arrival, he builds a boma, a wide corral with
a strong fence where the elephants can live while they get used
to their new home. He repairs broken spots in the outer fence.

Then he posts signs, reminding the neighboring Zulu villagers,

NO HUNTING.

Meanwhile, the elephants ride in a trailer, past sycamore figs and acacia trees, beyond the Umfolozi swamp, and along the Nseleni River.

They bump over one . . . two . . . three railway tracks and then down a dirt path where a sign points the way to Thula Thula.

The elephants **COME.**

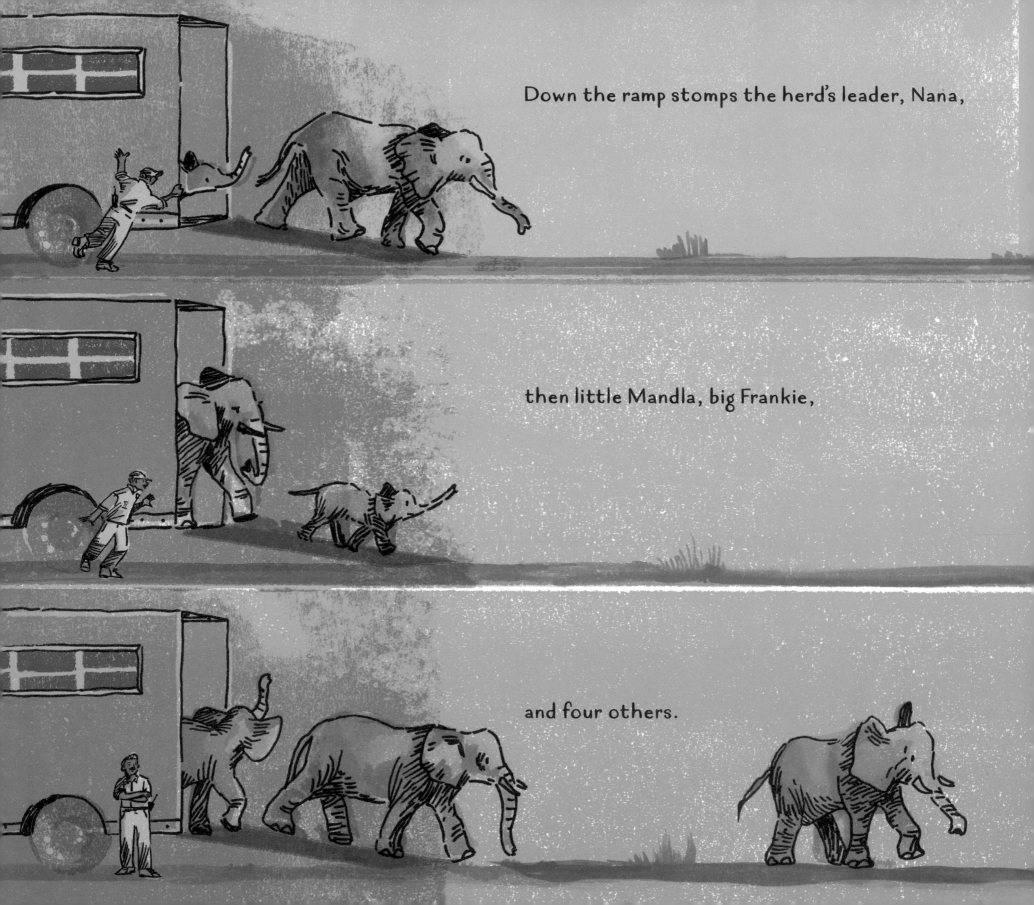

Down the ramp stomps the herd's leader, Nana,

then little Mandla, big Frankie,

and four others.

They look at the unfamiliar farmhouse, its swimming pool, and the boma. They look at the strangers—Lawrence, Françoise, and the rangers.

Right away the elephants pound
their hooves and trumpet angrily.

"They're **NAUGHTY**," the rangers complain.

"They're **NERVOUS**," Lawrence says.
"Wouldn't you be if you moved far from
your home?"

Everyone holds a breath and waits.

Finally, the elephants calm their noises and tromp into the boma.

That night, while Lawrence and Françoise sleep, Nana and Frankie heave their heads against a giant tamboti tree. They push and shove until the tree topples and smashes the boma fence.

The elephants bulldoze forward and use their bodies to break the outer fence. **CRASH!** The herd marches out of Thula Thula.

At sunrise, a worker cries,

"The elephants are **GONE**!"

Oh no!

Lawrence looks for the herd
by the Nseleni River.

Françoise and Max look by the Gwala Gwala dam.

Word spreads, and others look for them, too—hunters! Danger waits for the elephants outside the safety of Thula Thula.

Lawrence's friend Peter has a helicopter and searches the thick jungle from the sky. **EUREKA!** He spots the elephants in a grove of acacia trees.

Still, the emergency isn't over—he has to convince the elephants to turn around. **FAST**! They are walking closer and closer to dangerous territory.

Peter zooms close to the elephants over and over
again, trying to herd them away. The elephants are
unimpressed. But finally, inch by inch, the elephants
turn back to Thula Thula.

Back in the boma, the elephants bellow, throw dust, and flatten their ears.

"They're **DANGEROUS**," say the rangers.

"They're **SAD**," says Françoise.

"They're **STILL SCARED**," says Lawrence.

The herd approaches the repaired boma fence, ready to knock it down again, but Lawrence stands in front of them.

"Nana," Lawrence says. "**PLEASE** don't go. If you leave, you, your baby, and your herd will be hurt."

Nana curls her trunk and lifts her ears.

"Maybe you're worried about this new home and tired from the journey," Lawrence says.

"But if you rest, I'll take care of you. I will live with you by day and camp with you by night. I will stay with you, and you will not be alone."

Nana meets Lawrence's eyes for a moment.
Then she turns away from the fence
and leads the herd into the boma's brush.

The elephants stay.

Lawrence builds a tent, and he
and Max camp by the boma.
He sings to the elephants during the
day and tells them stories at night.

Soon the elephants' cranky behavior changes to ear flopping, head waggling, and trumpeting.

"What does it mean?" Françoise asks.

"They're **HAPPY**," Lawrence says.

Lawrence and Nana get to know each other. They walk together and talk together, Lawrence with words, Nana with comfortable rumbles.

One morning, Nana does something very special—
she reaches her trunk through the gate and pats
Lawrence's stomach. It is a sign of friendship.
Lawrence knows he can trust the elephants now.

At last, he opens the boma gates wide, so the elephants can explore the pastures, rivers, and thickets of Thula Thula.

The herd wanders off into the hills. They will graze
the savannas. They will splash and play. They are **HOME**.

Lawrence and Max move back into the house, and the elephants stroll to the lawn for regular visits.

Nana likes eating from Françoise's garden, swimming in the pool,

and clomping on the porch to pat Lawrence's stomach.

And whenever Lawrence goes away, somehow the herd knows the exact moment of his return.

They always come to the house just in time to welcome him home.

Years go by, and the elephants spend more and more time far away,
in the part of Thula Thula where the best acacia trees grow,
a twelve-hour journey from Lawrence and Françoise's house.

Lawrence and Françoise continue to live in
the farmhouse, sweeping spitting snakes,
tiptoeing around webs, and loving Max.

Françoise's garden grows lush, and
Lawrence's beard speckles with gray.

The rhinos splash in the river, the Cape buffalo graze the savanna,

and the crocodiles at the Gwala Gwala dam swim in peace.

Every few years, Nana and the herd come for a visit.

Then, one sunny
summer day,
Lawrence dies.

Somehow, deep in the brush of Thula Thula, the elephants know.

They begin their trek toward Lawrence's home that very day.
They journey past the Nseleni River and by the sycamore figs,
across the savanna and beyond the Gwala Gwala dam.

They **WALK**, and they **WALK**.

The elephants come.

Françoise looks out her window as the herd forms a circle around the house. The elephants look at Françoise, make soft rumbles, and bow their heads. They spend the next three days there.

The elephants live with Françoise
by day and camp with her by night.

They stay with her, and she is not alone.

AUTHOR'S NOTE

Lawrence Anthony died on March 2, 2012. For the next three years, the herd returned to the Anthony home on the exact anniversary of Lawrence's death.

The elephants continue to thrive, and there are children and grandchildren of the original seven elephants now living at Thula Thula. In March 2014, a 10-day-old elephant got separated from the herd. The tiny calf walked for three miles on her own, all the way to the farmhouse, where she was found in Françoise's mulberry bush. To read more, please check out *An Elephant in My Kitchen: What the Herd Taught Me About Love, Courage and Survival* by Françoise Malby-Anthony and Katja Willemsen.

Thula Thula is a wildlife sanctuary dedicated to the conservation, protection, and survival of endangered species. It has an expansion project for elephants as well as a rhinoceros orphanage. To learn more about Thula Thula's charity fund, please visit thulathula.com.

Nana and family   Photo credit: Kim McLeod

Lawrence at Thula Thula   Photo credit: Christopher Laurenz

ACKNOWLEDGMENTS

Thanks to Françoise Malby-Anthony for being an eco-warrior and for the work you do at Thula Thula. Thank you for providing photos; for answering my many emails, phone calls, and Facebook messages; and thanks for agreeing to an in-person interview with my proxies. Thanks to Steve Tomsic and Peggy Tomsic for traveling to Thula Thula, armed with my list of questions and photo requests. It's such a treat to know that Nana showed up to greet you during your last day on the reserve. I was delighted you returned with rich bonus information, such as the fact that Nana and her offspring share the genetic marker of having slightly crooked tails.

Thanks to Hadley Hooper for your gorgeous and special art.

Thanks to Stephen Mooser and Lin Oliver. I will be forever grateful that you created the SCBWI as a networking and gathering place for children's book writers and illustrators. The SCBWI opens doors, moves mountains, and connects people. At an SCBWI event I met Leni Checkas, who was the first person (outside my family) to offer encouragement. Because of Leni, I attended Andrea Brown's Big Sur in the Rockies Children's Book Writing Workshop, and then the SCBWI International Summer Conference where I met my

editor and my agent (drumroll, please), the dynamic duo—Melissa Manlove and Jen Rofé! Melissa, thank you for pushing me to find the heart of this story. Thanks to team Chronicle—Indya McGuffin, Amelia Mack, Ashley Despain, Aki Neumann, Claire Fletcher, Jamie Real, Feather Flores, Andie Krawczyk, Eva Zimmerman, Mary Duke, Samantha Chambers, Kaitlyn Spotts, and Carrie Gao—for all the behind-the-scenes work that went into making this book accurate, beautiful, and well-loved.

Thanks to Marjorie Tomsic for your day-one enthusiasm. Thank you, first readers: Linda Arms White, Steve Tomsic, Aspen Nolan, Renée Berberian, Katie Salidas, Celia Sinoway, Peggy Tomsic, Cindy Bateman, Anna Harber Freeman, Janet Mountain, and Jackson Mountain. Thank you for your support: David Deen, Barry Solway, Todd Tuell, and Jerilyn Patterson. Thank you to my brilliant critiquing partners, without whom I would not have a writing career: Elaine Pease, Will James Limón, Penny Berman, Sally Spear, Brian Papa, Denise Vega, Lauren Sabel, and Carissa Mina.

And thank you Steve, Noelle, and Cayman, for cheering me on through this process.

WORKS CITED

Anthony, Lawrence, and Graham Spence. *The Elephant Whisperer: My Life with the Herd in the African Wild.* New York: St. Martin's Griffin, 2012.

Aydin, Diane. "Elephants Remember the Man Who Saved Them." *Guideposts,* July 23, 2018, https://www.guideposts.org/tell-your-story/our-favorite-stories/elephants-remember-the-man-who-saved-them.

"Elephant Call Types Database." ElephantVoices, https://www.elephantvoices.org/multimedia-resources/elephant-call-types-database.html.

Françoise Malby-Anthony. Interview by Steve Tomsic and Peggy Tomsic, April 8, 2017.

Frei, Georges. "Communication between Elephants Voices and Sounds." Elephants in Zoo and Circus Elephant Encyclopedia. Upali, http://www.upali.ch/communication_en.html.

"Lawrence Anthony's Rehabilitation of Elephants." YouTube, March 24, 2009, https://www.youtube.com/watch?v=F4nvQbfQAUg.

Malby-Anthony, Françoise. "Françoise Malby-Anthony—Encounters with Elephants." Ideacity, June 2014, http://www.ideacityonline.com/video/encounters-elephants-francoise-malby-anthony/.

Moorhead, Joanna. "What Elephants Can Teach Us about Love." *Sydney Morning Herald,* June 18, 2009, https://www.smh.com.au/environment/conservation/what-elephants-can-teach-us-about-love-20090617-chyi.html.

O'Connell-Rodwell, Caitlin. "Keeping an 'Ear' to the Ground: Seismic Communication in Elephants." *American Physiological Society* 22, no. 4 (2007): 287-294.

Siebert, Charles. "The Lives They Lived": Lawrence Anthony. *The New York Times,* December 28, 2012, http://archive.nytimes.com/www.nytimes.com/interactive/2012/12/30/magazine/the-lives-they-lived-2012.html?view=Lawrence_Anthony.

"Trunk Call: How Elephants Communicate Using a 'Secret Language.'" *Daily Mail,* February 22, 2010, https://www.dailymail.co.uk/sciencetech/article-1252912/Elephants-communicate-using-secret-language.html.

"UPDATE: Elephants Who Appeared to Mourn Their Human Friend Remain Protected." *CBC News Canada,* July 25, 2012, https://www.cbc.ca/strombo/news/saying-goodbye-elephants-hold-apparent-vigil-to-mourn-their-human-friend.ht.

Library of Congress Cataloging-in-Publication Data:

Names: Tomsic, Kim, author. | Hooper, Hadley, illustrator.

Title: The elephants come home : a true story of seven elephants,
  two people, and one extraordinary friendship / Kim Tomsic,
  Hadley Hooper.

Description: San Francisco: Chronicle Books, 2021. | Includes
  bibliographical references. | Audience: Ages 3-5 | Audience: Grades
  2-3 | Summary: "Lawrence Anthony and Françoise Malby-Anthony
  love animals—so when they hear that a herd of wild African
  elephants needs a new home, they welcome the herd to their
  wildlife sanctuary—Thula Thula—with open arms. What follows in
  this beautifully illustrated true story is an extraordinary cross-
  species friendship that will move readers and warm the hearts of
  animal lovers at every age"— Provided by publisher.

Identifiers: LCCN 2020017908 | ISBN 9781452127835 (hardcover)

Subjects: LCSH: Animal welfare—Juvenile literature. | Human-
  animal relationships—Juvenile literature. | Elephants—
  Juvenile literature.

Classification: LCC HV4708 .T65 2021 | DDC
  333.95/96716096842—dc23LC record available at
  https://lccn.loc.gov/2020017908

Manufactured in China.

Design by Indya McGuffin.

Art Direction by Amelia Mack and Indya McGuffin.

Typeset in Quimbly.

The illustrations in the book were created
by using watercolor, ink, printmaking, and
then finished in Photoshop.

10 9 8 7 6 5 4 3

Chronicle Books LLC
680 Second Street
San Francisco, California 94107

Chronicle Books—we see things differently. Become
part of our community at www.chroniclekids.com.